MW01492927

SPECTRUM®

Lowercase Letters

PreK–K

Published by Spectrum®
an imprint of Carson-Dellosa Publishing
Greensboro, NC

Spectrum®
An imprint of Carson-Dellosa Publishing LLC
P.O. Box 35665
Greensboro, NC 27425 USA

ISBN 978-1-4838-3100-8

01-053167784

Table of Contents

Recognizing Lowercase Letters

Writing Lowercase Letters

a b c d e f g h i j k l m n o p q r s t u v w x y z

Find a

Directions: Help the ant find the picnic. Color the boxes with **a**.

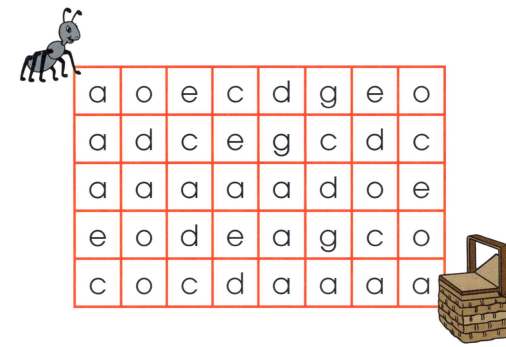

a	o	e	c	d	g	e	o
a	d	c	e	g	c	d	c
a	a	a	a	a	d	o	e
e	o	d	e	a	g	c	o
c	o	c	d	a	a	a	a

Directions: Circle **a** in each word.

apple   hat

a **b** c d e f g h i j k l m n o p q r s t u v w x y z

Find b

Directions: Color the shapes with **b**.

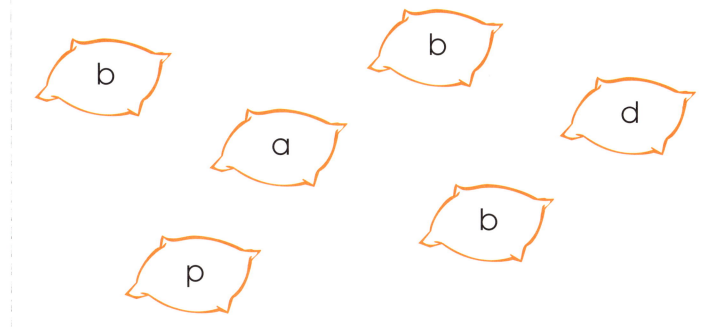

Directions: Circle **b** in each word.

book

bear

a b **c** d e f g h i j k l m n o p q r s t u v w x y z

Find c

Directions: Draw a line from the corn to the circles with **c**.

Directions: Circle **c** in each word.

cat

sock

a b c **d** e f g h i j k l m n o p q r s t u v w x y z

Find d

  **d**og

Directions: Help the dog find the bone. Color the boxes with **d**.

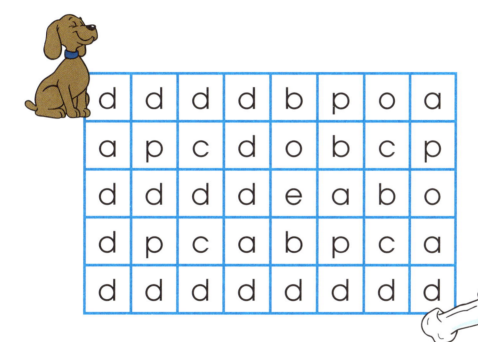

d	d	d	d	b	p	o	a
a	p	c	d	o	b	c	p
d	d	d	d	e	a	b	o
d	p	c	a	b	p	c	a
d	d	d	d	d	d	d	d

Directions: Circle **d** in each word.

deer

red

a b c d **e** f g h i j k l m n o p q r s t u v w x y z

Find e

  **egg**

Directions: Color the shapes with **e**.

Directions: Circle **e** in each word.

ten

bell

a b c d e **f** g h i j k l m n o p q r s t u v w x y z

Find f

Directions: Draw a line from the feather to the circles with **f**.

Directions: Circle **f** in each word.

five

leaf

a b c d e f **g** h i j k l m n o p q r s t u v w x y z

Find g

Directions: Help the girl win the game. Color the boxes with **g**.

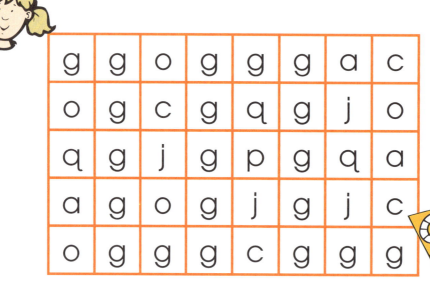

g	g	o	g	g	g	a	c
o	g	c	g	q	g	j	o
q	g	j	g	p	g	q	a
a	g	o	g	j	g	j	c
o	g	g	g	c	g	g	g

Directions: Circle **g** in each word.

guitar

rug

a b c d e f g **h** i j k l m n o p q r s t u v w x y z

Find h

  **h**orse

Directions: Color the shapes with **h**.

 n

 h

 p

 m

 h

 h

Directions: Circle **h** in each word.

house

horn

a b c d e f g h **i** j k l m n o p q r s t u v w x y z

Find i

Directions: Draw a line from the igloo to the circles with **i**.

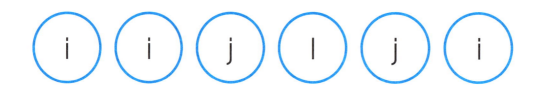

Directions: Circle **i** in each word.

ink

six

a b c d e f g h i **j** k l m n o p q r s t u v w x y z

Find j

Directions: Help the jet fly. Start at the bottom. Color the boxes with **j**.

j	j	g	q	i	g	p	i
i	j	j	j	t	i	b	l
g	b	t	j	j	p	i	g
l	t	g	b	j	j	q	p
i	q	p	l	g	j	j	j

Directions: Circle **j** in each word.

jacket

jar

a b c d e f g h i j **k** l m n o p q r s t u v w x y z

Find k

  **kite**

Directions: Color the shapes with **k**.

Directions: Circle **k** in each word.

key

lock

a b c d e f g h i j k **l** m n o p q r s t u v w x y z

Find l

 **l**

  **l**ion

Directions: Draw a line from the ladder to the circles with **l**.

l   k   t   l   f   l

Directions: Circle **l** in each word.

letters

mailbox

a b c d e f g h i j k l **m** n o p q r s t u v w x y z

Find m

Directions: Help the rocket get to the moon. Start at the bottom. Color the boxes with **m**.

m	h	b	n	v	w	r	n
r	m	r	h	w	n	r	w
n	w	m	r	h	w	h	b
w	v	b	m	v	h	w	n
n	r	h	w	m	m	m	m

Directions: Circle **m** in each word.

mouse

drum

a b c d e f g h i j k l m **n** o p q r s t u v w x y z

Find n

  **n**est

Directions: Color the shapes with **n**.

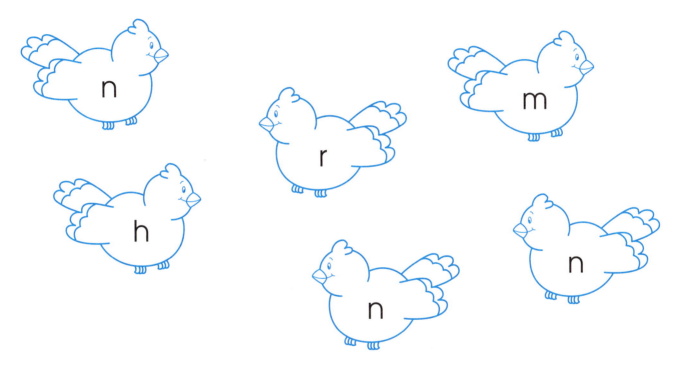

Directions: Circle **n** in each word.

nut

9

nine

a b c d e f g h i j k l m n **o** p q r s t u v w x y z

Find o

  **octopus**

Directions: Draw a line from the octopus to the circles with **o**.

Directions: Circle **o** in each word.

olives

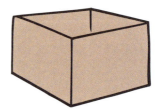

box

a b c d e f g h i j k l m n o **p** q r s t u v w x y z

Find p

 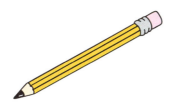 **p**encil

Directions: Help the pencil write on the paper. Color the boxes with **p**.

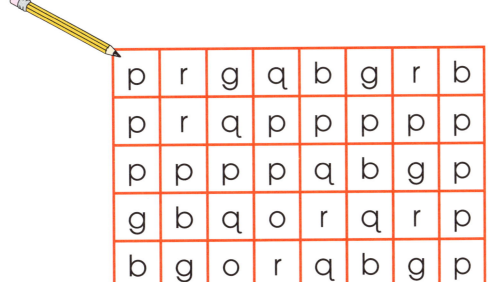

Directions: Circle **p** in each word.

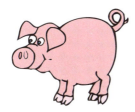

pig

mop

a b c d e f g h i j k l m n o p **q** r s t u v w x y z

Find q

  **quilt**

Directions: Color the shapes with **q**.

Directions: Circle **q** in each word.

quarter

quack

a b c d e f g h i j k l m n o p q **r** s t u v w x y z

Find r

  **r**ainbow

Directions: Draw a line from the raindrops to the circles with **r**.

h   r   r   r   n   m

Directions: Circle **r** in each word.

ring

car

Find s

Directions: Help the sun shine on the flower. Color the boxes with **s**.

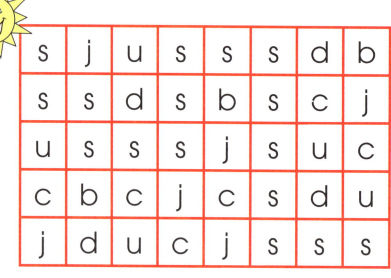

s	j	u	s	s	s	d	b
s	s	d	s	b	s	c	j
u	s	s	s	j	s	u	c
c	b	c	j	c	s	d	u
j	d	u	c	j	s	s	s

Directions: Circle **s** in each word.

hose

bus

a b c d e f g h i j k l m n o p q r s **t** u v w x y z

Find t

  **tent**

Directions: Color the shapes with **t**.

Directions: Circle **t** in each word.

turtle   nut

a b c d e f g h i j k l m n o p q r s t **u** v w x y z

Find u

  **u**mbrella

Directions: Draw a line from the umbrella to the circles with **u**.

n   u   h   u   u   s

Directions: Circle **u** in each word.

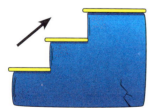

up

mug

a b c d e f g h i j k l m n o p q r s t u **v** w x y z

Find v

van

Directions: Help the van get home. Color the boxes with **v**.

v	w	n	m	v	v	v	v
v	n	w	y	v	w	n	v
v	w	y	m	v	m	m	v
v	v	v	v	v	w	y	v
m	w	n	x	w	m	n	v

Directions: Circle **v** in each word.

vase

vest

a b c d e f g h i j k l m n o p q r s t u v **W** x y z

Find w

web

Directions: Color the shapes with **w**.

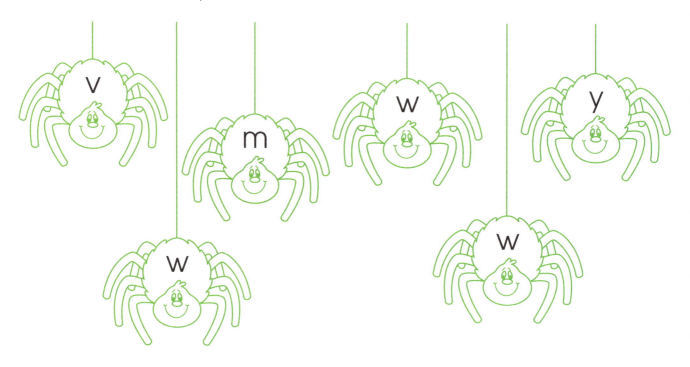

Directions: Circle **w** in each word.

worm

well

a b c d e f g h i j k l m n o p q r s t u v w **x** y z

Find x

fo**x**

Directions: Draw a line from the fox to the circles with **x**.

Directions: Circle **x** in each word.

six

ax

a b c d e f g h i j k l m n o p q r s t u v w x **y** z

Find y

  **yarn**

Directions: Color the shapes with **y**.

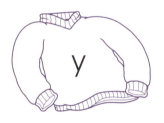 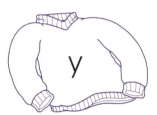

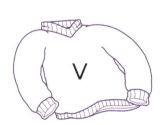

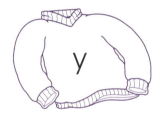 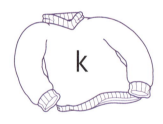

Directions: Circle **y** in each word.

yard

yo-yo

a b c d e f g h i j k l m n o p q r s t u v w x y **z**

Find z

  **z**ebra

Directions: Help the zebra get to the zoo. Color the boxes with **z**.

z	x	k	v	y	f	k	y
z	z	z	z	k	v	x	k
y	w	x	z	z	z	z	z
x	y	f	s	v	k	w	z
k	v	x	y	k	x	y	z

Directions: Circle **z** in each word.

zipper

puzzle

a b c d e f g h i j k l m n o p q r s t u v w x y z

Review

Directions: In each row, circle the letter that is the same as the first letter in the row.

a	m	a	h	c
d	t	o	d	r
k	w	d	t	k
f	h	t	p	f
q	q	o	g	m
c	o	z	c	g
s	w	s	m	a

a b c d e f g h i j k l m n o p q r s t u v w x y z

Review

Directions: In each row, circle the letter that is the same as the first letter in the row.

g	c	g	q	o
p	d	p	b	r
t	f	t	l	i
y	y	v	z	w
u	h	r	u	n
w	n	v	m	w
v	v	a	y	n

a b c d e f g h i j k l m n o p q r s t u v w x y z

I Know My abc's

Directions: Name the letters and pictures. Circle the letter in each word.

a apple

b bee

c sock

d sled

e egg

f fish

g flag

h hat

i milk

j jam

k kangaroo

l plate

m monkey

a b c d e f g h i j k l m n o p q r s t u v w x y z

I Know My abc's

Directions: Name the letters and pictures. Circle the letter in each word.

n pan

o doll

p tape

q queen

r frog

s saw

t tiger

u bus

v vase

w snow

x box

y puppy

z zebra

a b c d e f g h i j k l m n o p q r s t u v w x y z

I Know My abc's

Directions: Help the bat find the cave. Connect the letters in abc order.

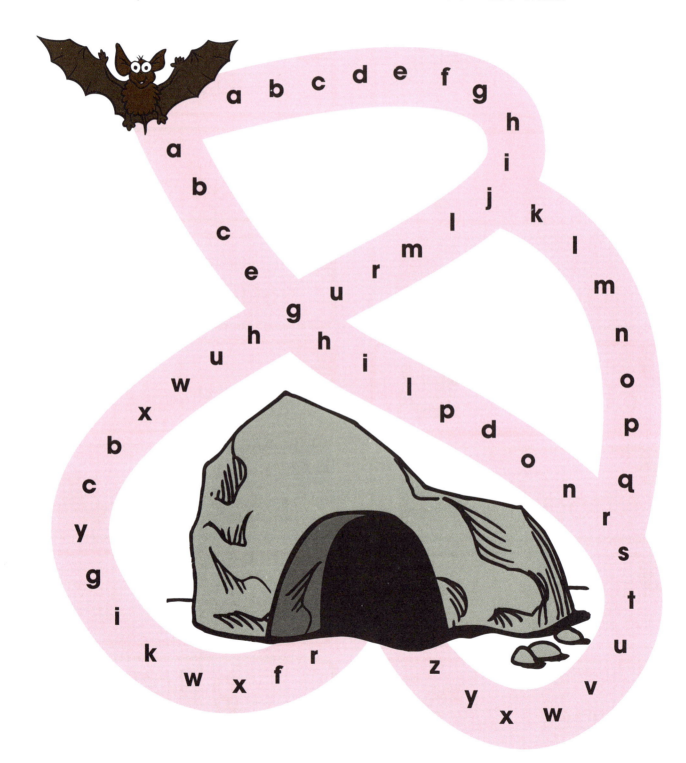

a b c d e f g h i j k l m n o p q r s t u v w x y z

I Know My abc's

Directions: Connect the dots in abc order.

a b c d e f g h i j k l m n o p q r s t u v w x y z

Write Lines From Top to Bottom

Directions: Trace each line from top to bottom. Begin at ●.

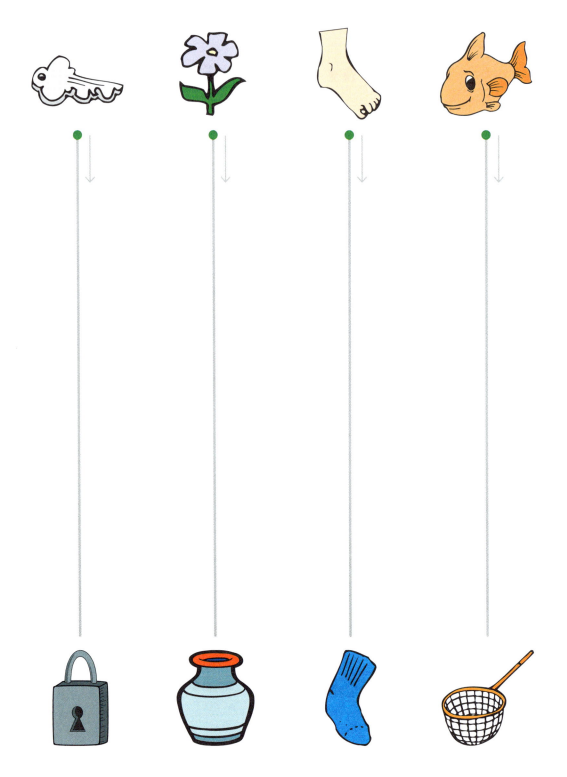

a b c d e f g h i j k l m n o p q r s t u v w x y z

Write Lines From Left to Right

Directions: Trace each line from left to right. Begin at ●.

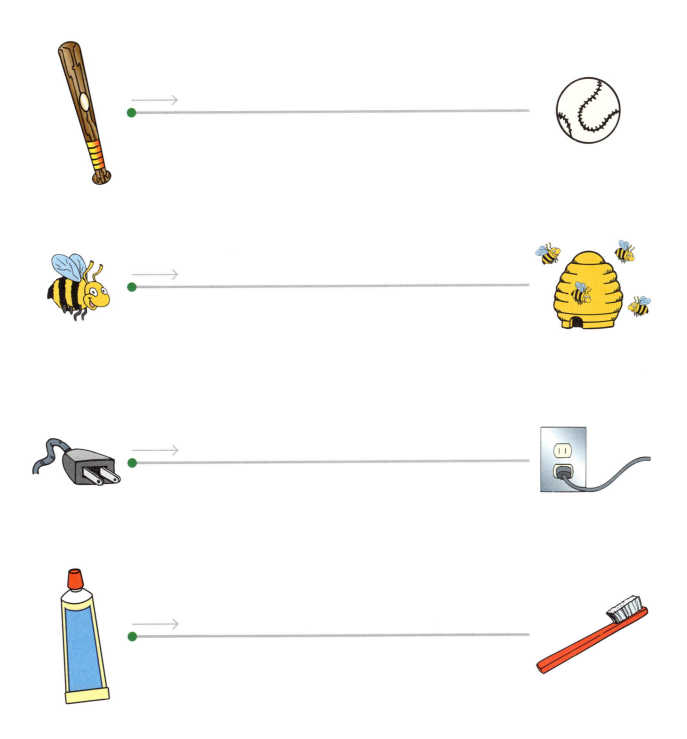

a b c d e f g h i j k **l** m n o p q r s t u v w x y z

Write l

Directions: Look at the letter and the arrows. Then, trace and write the letter. Begin at ●.

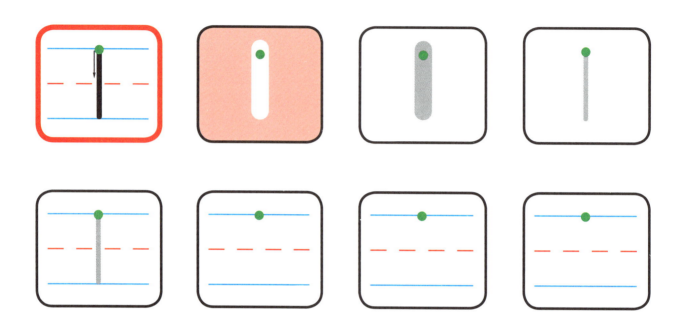

Directions: Write **l** to complete the words.

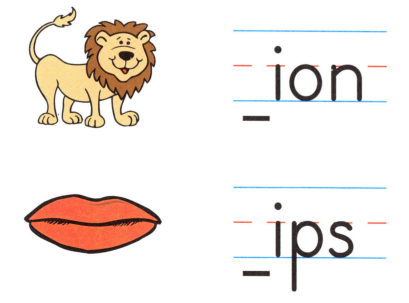

_l_ion

_l_ips

a b c d e f g h **i** j k l m n o p q r s t u v w x y z

Write i

Directions: Look at the letter and the arrows. Then, trace and write the letter. Begin at ●.

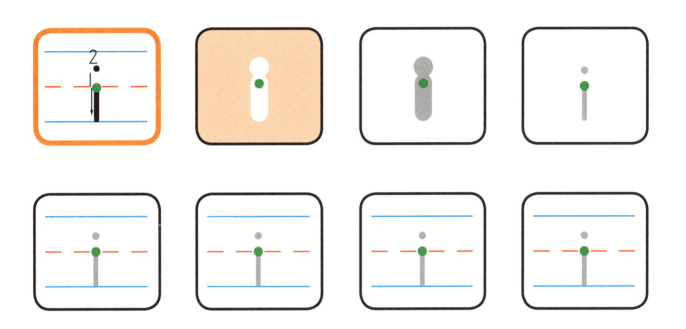

Directions: Write **i** to complete the words.

m_lk

f_sh

a b c d e f g h i j k l m n o p q r s **t** u v w x y z

Write t

Directions: Look at the letter and the arrows. Then, trace and write the letter. Begin at ●.

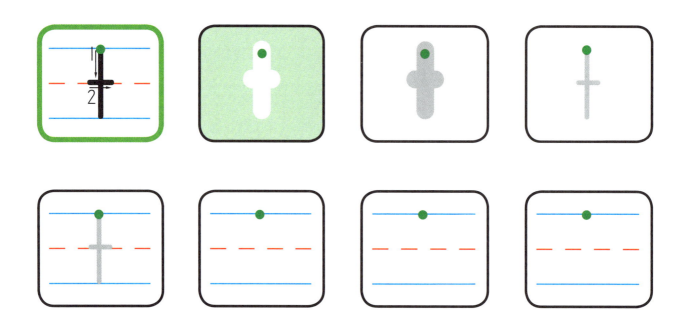

Directions: Write **t** to complete the words.

_omato

_op

a b c d e f g h i **j** k l m n o p q r s t u v w x y z

Write j

Directions: Look at the letter and the arrows. Then, trace and write the letter. Begin at ●.

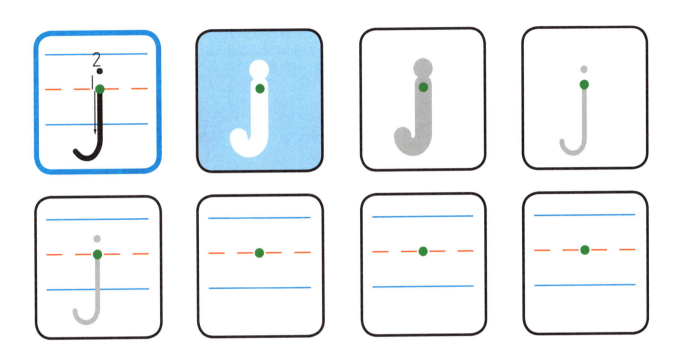

Directions: Write **j** to complete the words.

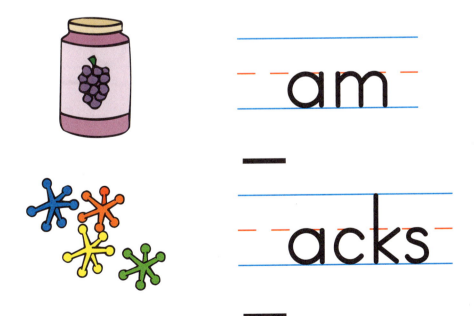

___am

___acks

a b c d e f g h i j k l m n o p q r s t u v w x y z

Review

Directions: Write a letter from the box to complete each word.

i	j	l	t

b b
_

eep
_

sea_
_

_iger

ca_
_

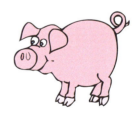

p_g

Write Backward Circles

Directions: Trace each circle. Begin at ●.

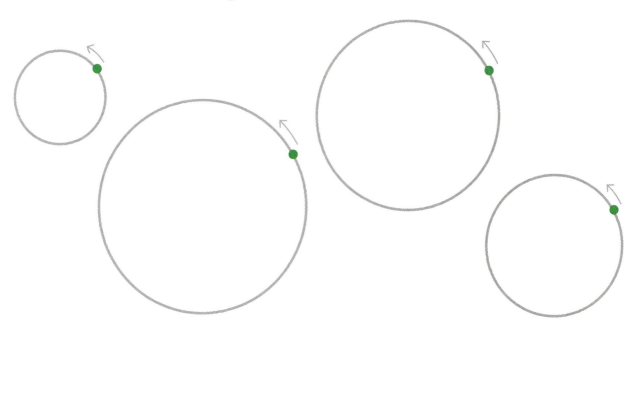

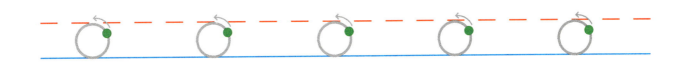

a b c d e f g h i j k l m n **o** p q r s t u v w x y z

Write o

Directions: Look at the letter and the arrows. Then, trace and write the letter. Begin at ●.

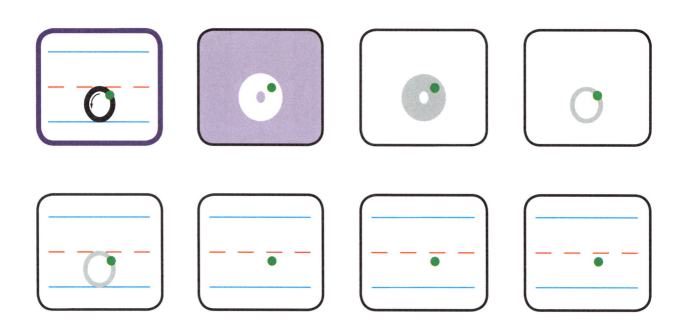

Directions: Write **o** to complete the words.

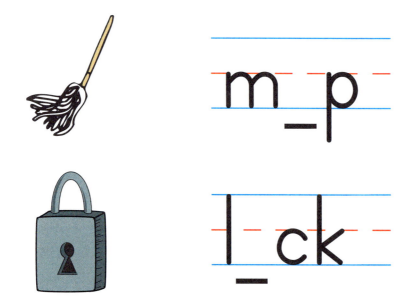

m_p

l_ck

a b c d e f g h i j k l m n o p q r s t u v w x y z

Write a

Directions: Look at the letter and the arrows. Then, trace and write the letter. Begin at ●.

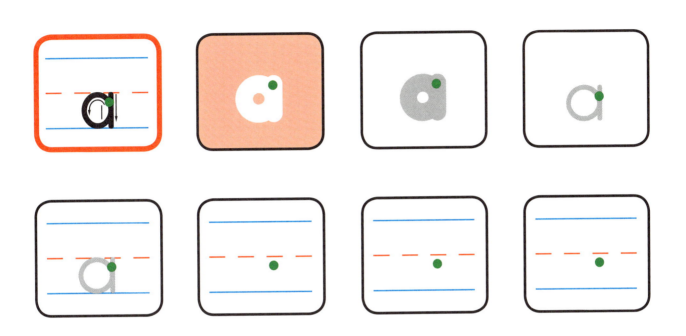

Directions: Write **a** to complete the words.

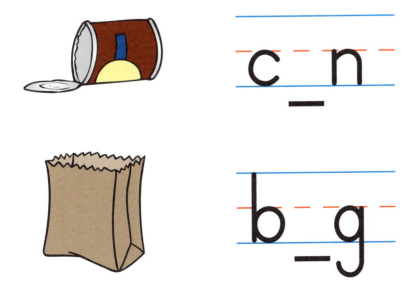

c _ n

b _ g

a b c **d** e f g h i j k l m n o p q r s t u v w x y z

Write d

Directions: Look at the letter and the arrows. Then, trace and write the letter. Begin at ●.

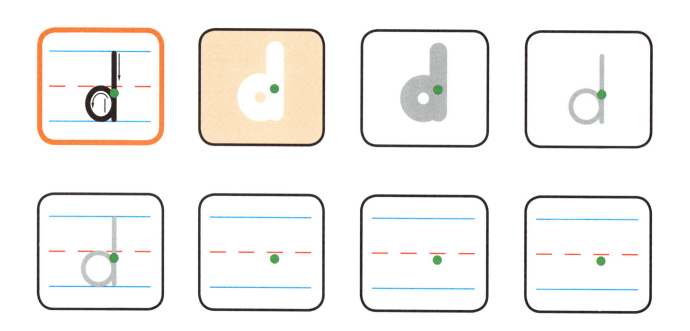

Directions: Write **d** to complete the words.

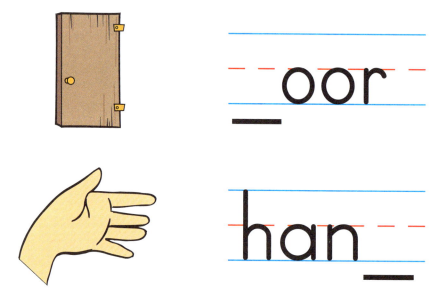

___oor

han___

a b **c** d e f g h i j k l m n o p q r s t u v w x y z

Write c

Directions: Look at the letter and the arrows. Then, trace and write the letter. Begin at ●.

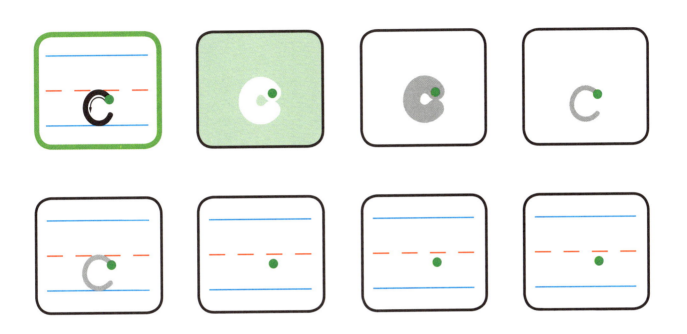

Directions: Write **c** to complete the words.

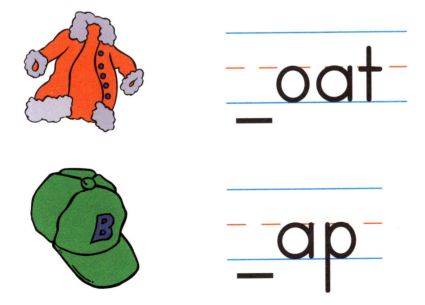

_oat

_ap

Name_____

a b c d **e** f g h i j k l m n o p q r s t u v w x y z

Write e

Directions: Look at the letter and the arrows. Then, trace and write the letter. Begin at ●.

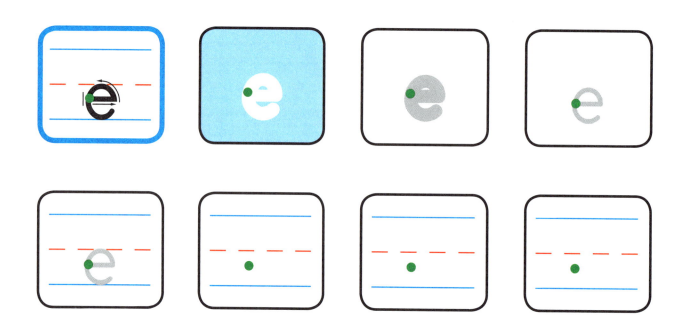

Directions: Write **e** to complete the words.

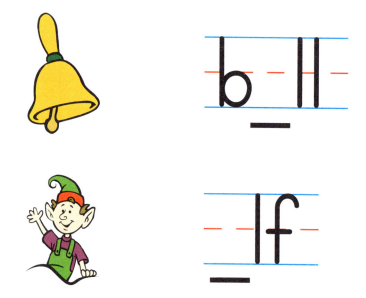

b_ll

_lf

a b c d e **f** g h i j k l m n o p q r s t u v w x y z

Write f

Directions: Look at the letter and the arrows. Then, trace and write the letter. Begin at ●.

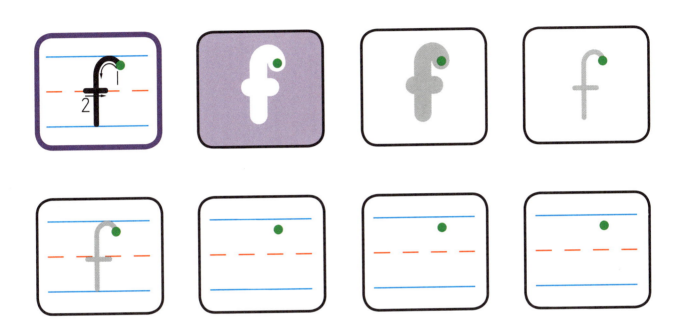

Directions: Write **f** to complete the words.

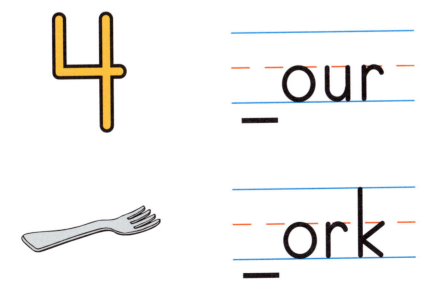

_our

_ork

a b c d e f **g** h i j k l m n o p q r s t u v w x y z

Write g

Directions: Look at the letter and the arrows. Then, trace and write the letter. Begin at ●.

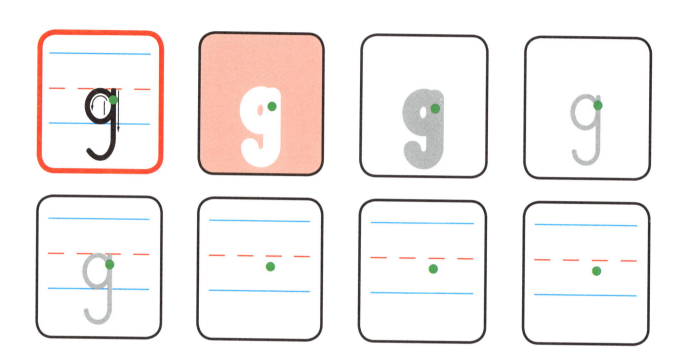

Directions: Write **g** to complete the words.

ru___

___as

Write q

Directions: Look at the letter and the arrows. Then, trace and write the letter. Begin at ●.

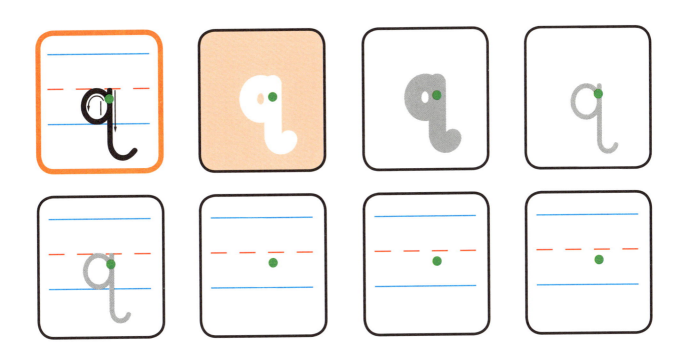

Directions: Write **q** to complete the words.

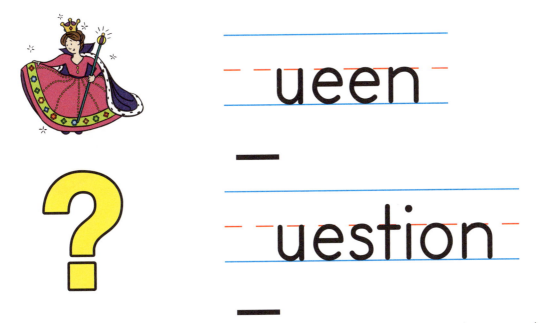

_ueen

_uestion

a b c d e f g h i j k l m n o p q r s t u v w x y z

Review

Directions: Write a letter from the box to complete each word.

a	c	d	e

do _ tor

n _ t

m _ p

_ andle

10

t _ n

_ _ ice

a b c d e f g h i j k l m n o p q r s t u v w x y z

Review

Directions: Write a letter from the box to complete each word.

f	g	o	q

___oose

g_at

___uarter

p_t

fro___

lea___

a b c d e f g h i j k l m n o p q r s t u v w x y z

Write Forward Circles

Directions: Trace each circle. Begin at ●.

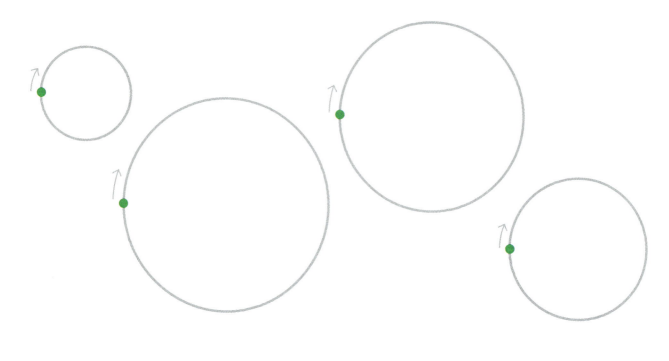

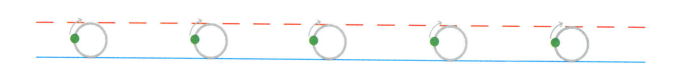

a b c d e f g h i j k l m n o p q r s t u v w x y z

Write Curved Lines

Directions: Trace the curved lines. Begin at ●.

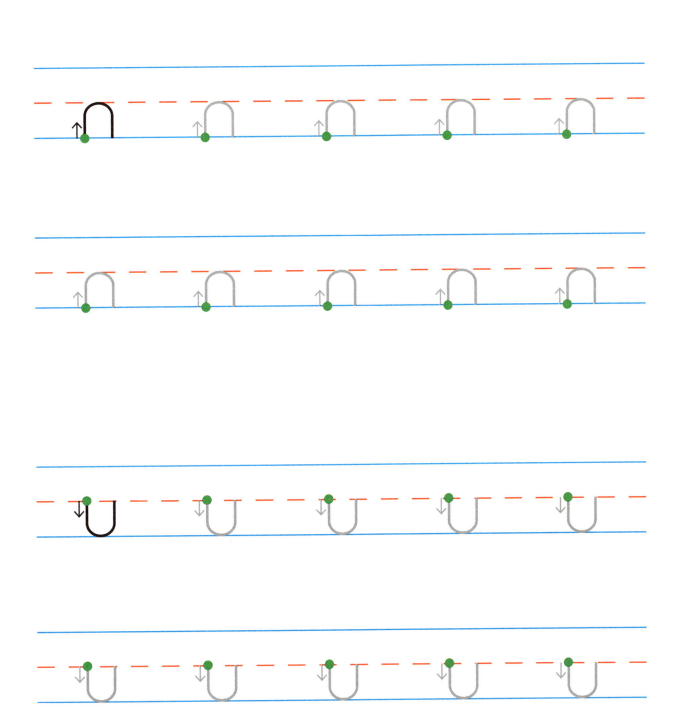

a **b** c d e f g h i j k l m n o p q r s t u v w x y z

Write b

Directions: Look at the letter and the arrows. Then, trace and write the letter. Begin at ●.

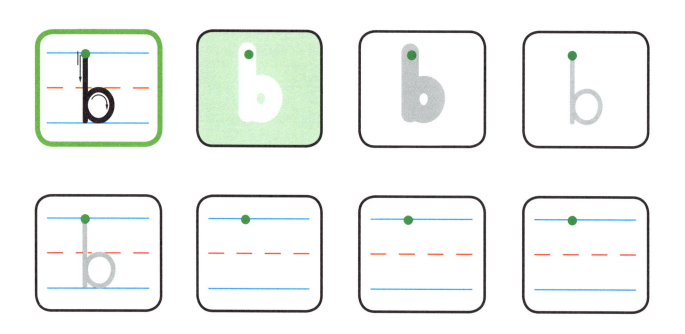

Directions: Write **b** to complete the words.

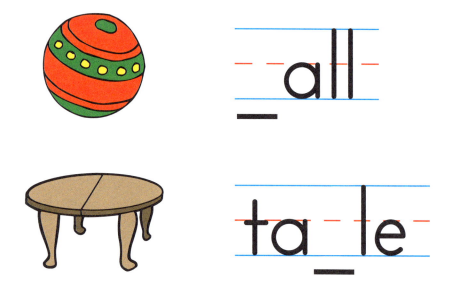

_all

ta_le

a b c d e f g h i j k l m n o **p** q r s t u v w x y z

Write p

Directions: Look at the letter and the arrows. Then, trace and write the letter. Begin at ●.

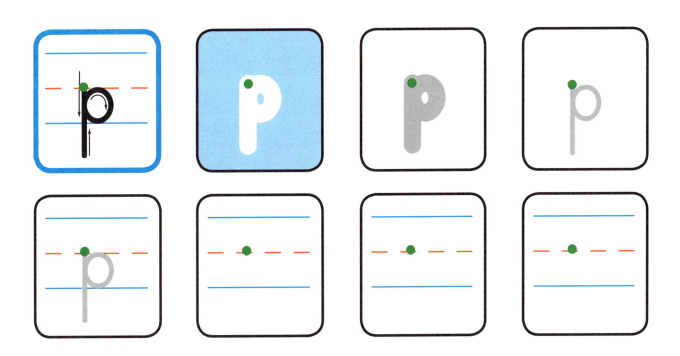

Directions: Write **p** to complete the words.

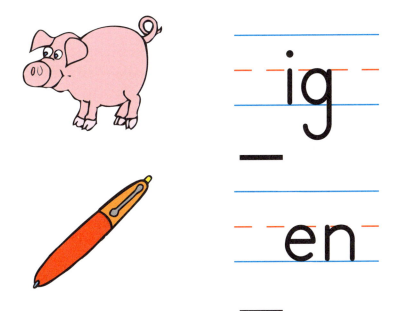

___ig

___en

a b c d e f g h i j k l m n o p q **r** s t u v w x y z

Write r

Directions: Look at the letter and the arrows. Then, trace and write the letter. Begin at ●.

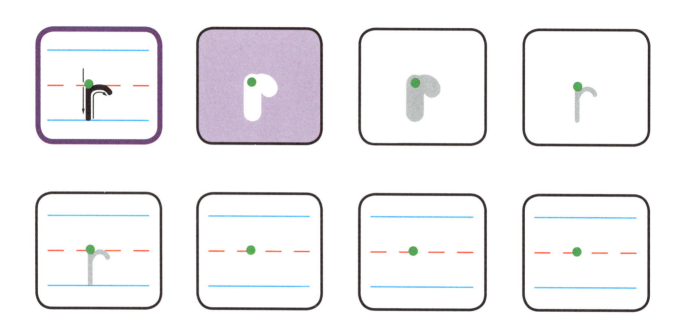

Directions: Write **r** to complete the words.

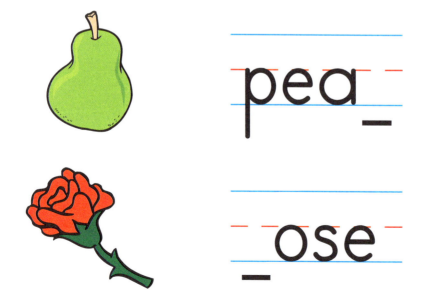

pea_

_ose

a b c d e f g h i j k l m **n** o p q r s t u v w x y z

Write n

Directions: Look at the letter and the arrows. Then, trace and write the letter. Begin at ●.

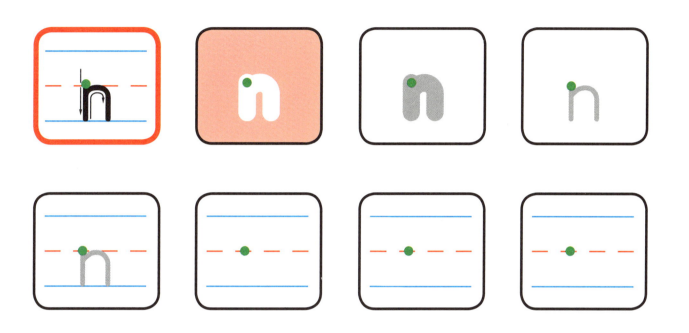

Directions: Write **n** to complete the words.

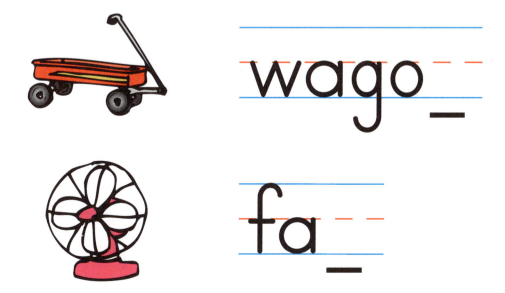

wago__

fa__

Write m

Directions: Look at the letter and the arrows. Then, trace and write the letter. Begin at ●.

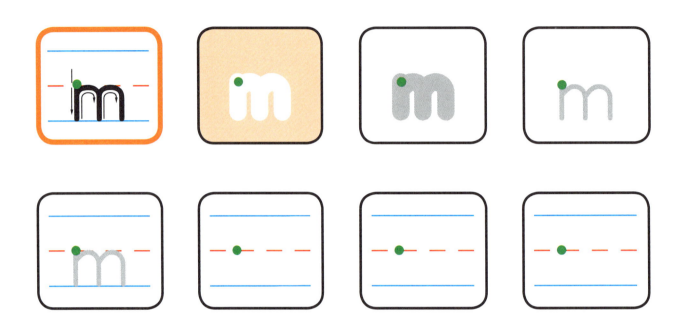

Directions: Write **m** to complete the words.

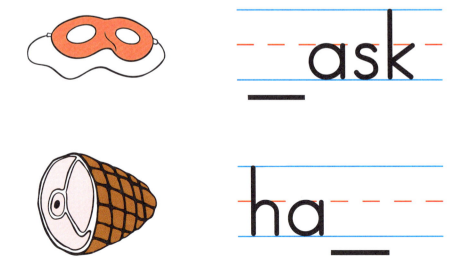

__ask

ha__

a b c d e f g **h** i j k l m n o p q r s t u v w x y z

Write h

Directions: Look at the letter and the arrows. Then, trace and write the letter. Begin at ●.

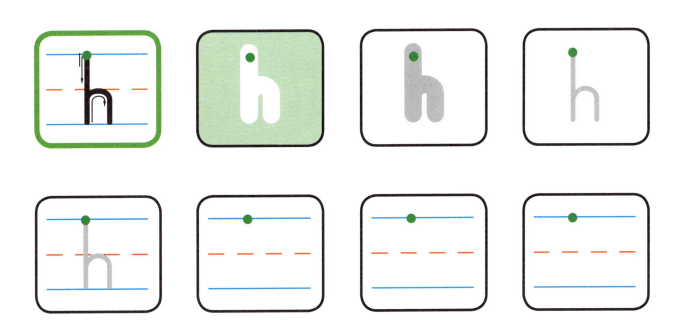

Directions: Write **h** to complete the words.

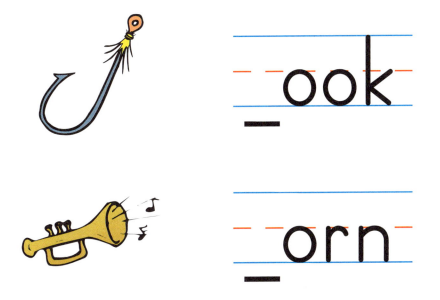

_ook

_orn

a b c d e f g h i j k l m n o p q r s t **u** v w x y z

Write u

Directions: Look at the letter and the arrows. Then, trace and write the letter. Begin at ●.

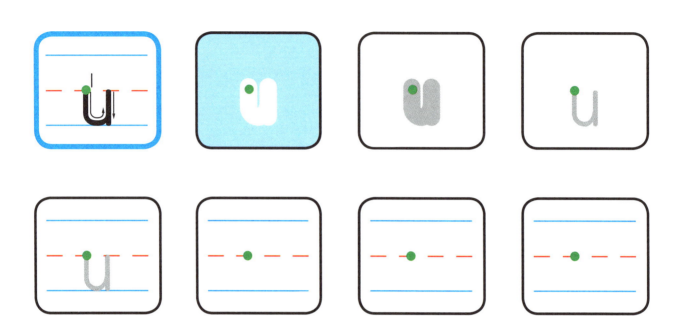

Directions: Write **u** to complete the words.

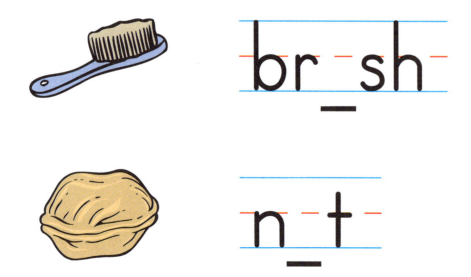

br_sh

n_t

a b c d e f g h i j k l m n o p q r S t u v w x y z

Write s

Directions: Look at the letter and the arrows. Then, trace and write the letter. Begin at ●.

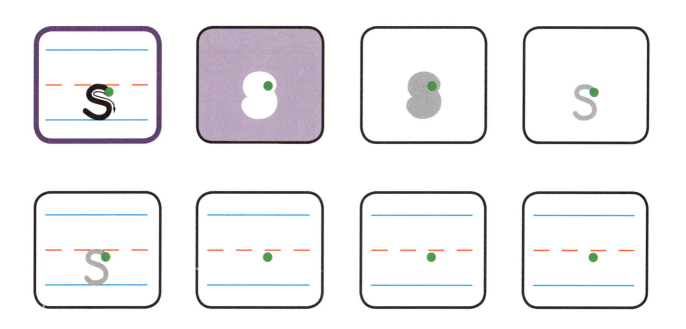

Directions: Write **s** to complete the words.

octopu_

even

a b c d e f g h i j k l m n o p q r s t u v w x y z

Review

Directions: Write letters from the box to complete the words.

| b | h | m | n | p | r | s | u |

__ __ __ s

__ oof

__ ose

__ oa __

__ umbers

__ oney

a b c d e f g h i j k l m n o p q r s t u v w x y z

Write Slanted Lines

Directions: Trace each line from top to bottom. Begin at ●.

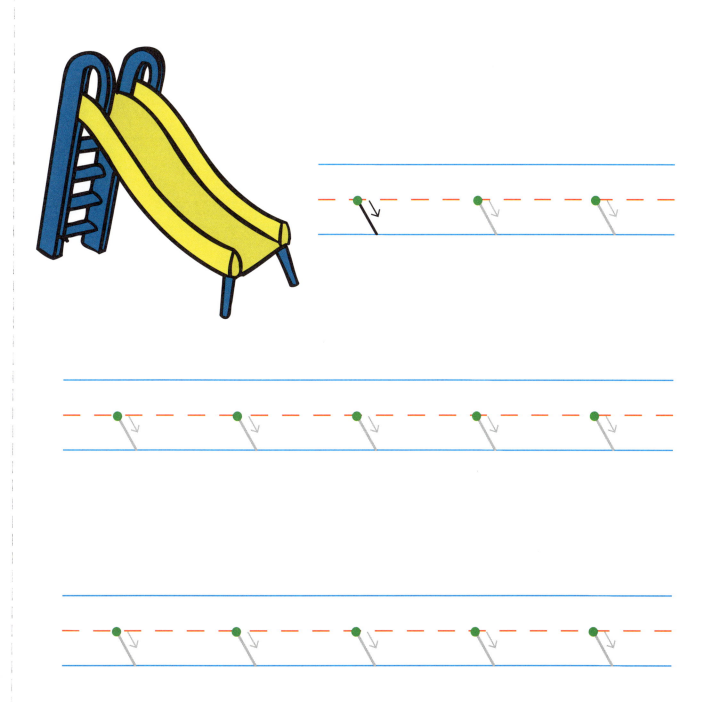

a b c d e f g h i j k l m n o p q r s t u v w x y z

Write Slanted Lines

Directions: Trace each line. Begin at ●.

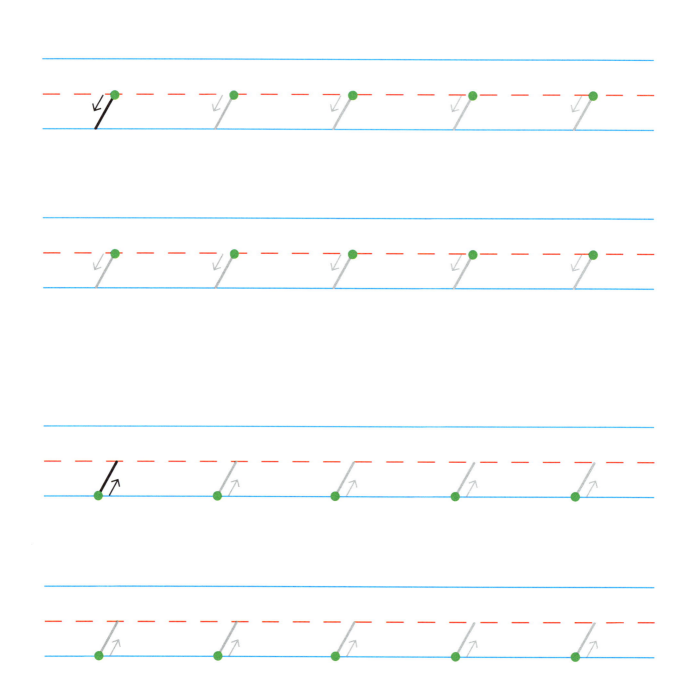

a b c d e f g h i j **k** l m n o p q r s t u v w x y z

Write k

Directions: Look at the letter and the arrows. Then, trace and write the letter. Begin at ●.

Directions: Write **k** to complete the words.

duc __

__ ing

a b c d e f g h i j k l m n o p q r s t u **v** w x y z

Write v

Directions: Look at the letter and the arrows. Then, trace and write the letter. Begin at ●.

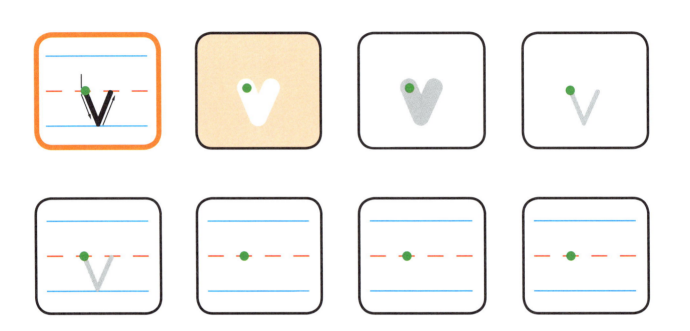

Directions: Write **v** to complete the words.

_ine

di_e

a b c d e f g h i j k l m n o p q r s t u v **w** x y z

Write w

Directions: Look at the letter and the arrows. Then, trace and write the letter. Begin at ●.

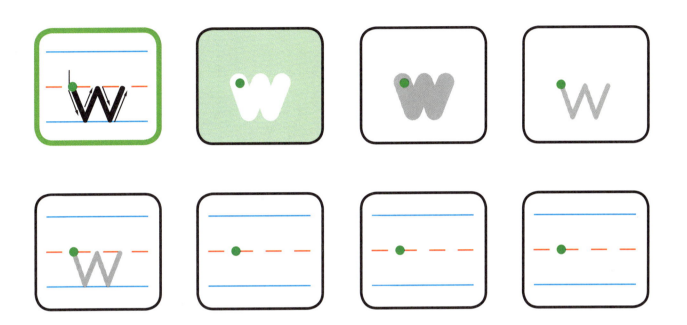

Directions: Write **w** to complete the words.

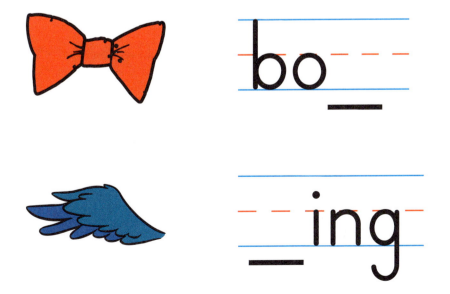

bo___

___ing

Write x

Directions: Look at the letter and the arrows. Then, trace and write the letter. Begin at ●.

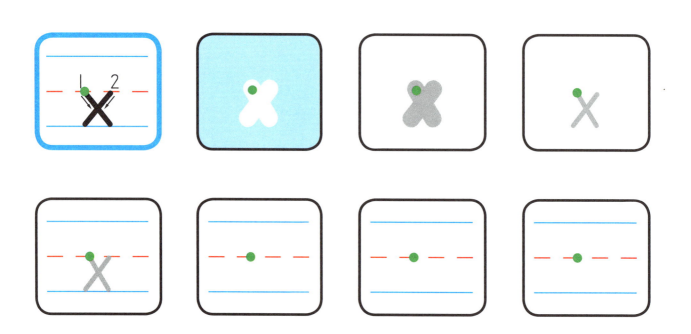

Directions: Write **x** to complete the words.

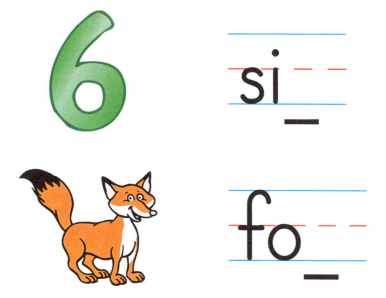

si___

fo___

a b c d e f g h i j k l m n o p q r s t u v w x **y** z

Write y

Directions: Look at the letter and the arrows. Then, trace and write the letter. Begin at ●.

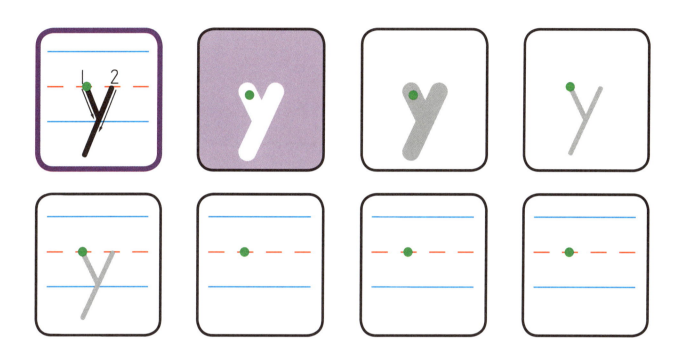

Directions: Write **y** to complete the words.

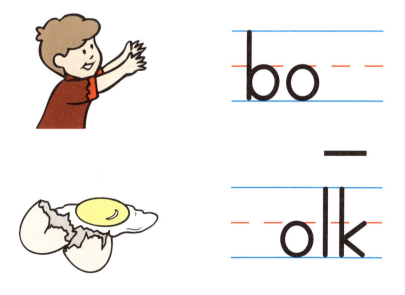

bo ___

___olk ___

Write z

Directions: Look at the letter and the arrows. Then, trace and write the letter. Begin at •.

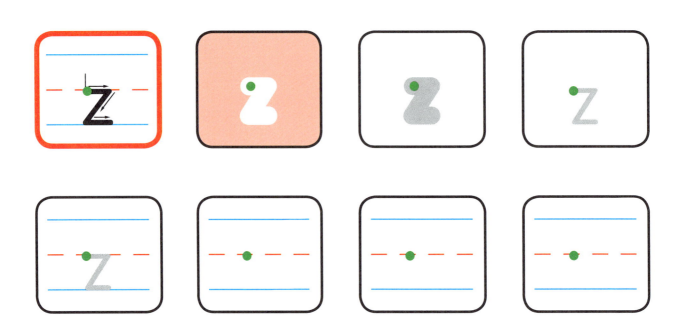

Directions: Write **z** to complete the words.

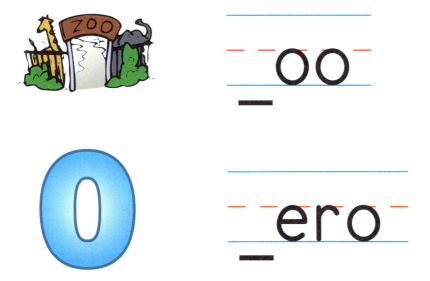

_oo

_ero

a b c d e f g h i j k l m n o p q r s t u v w x y z

Review

Directions: Write letters from the box to complete the words.

| k | v | w | x | y | z |

_an

bo_

soc_

_ipper

_arn

_orm

a b c d e f g h i j k l m n o p q r s t u v w x y z

Writing Review

Directions: Say the name of each picture. Write the lowercase letter that names its beginning sound.

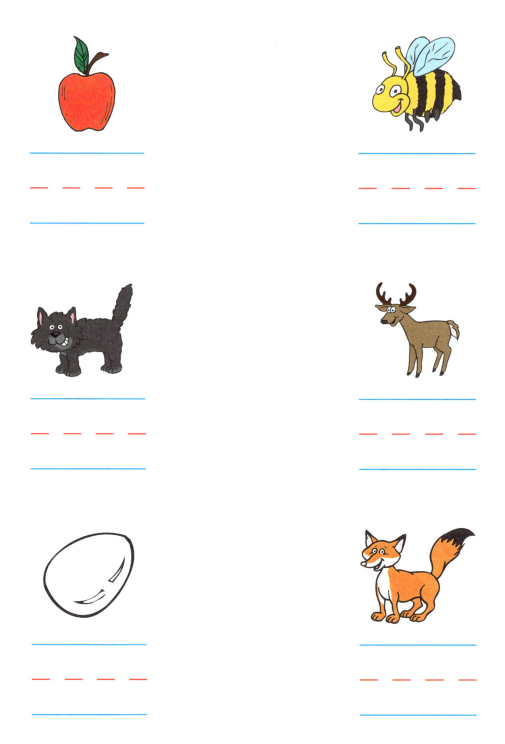

Writing Review

Directions: Say the name of each picture. Write the lowercase letter that names its beginning sound.

a b c d e f g h i j k l m n o p q r s t u v w x y z

Writing Review

Directions: Say the name of each picture. Write the lowercase letter that names its beginning sound.

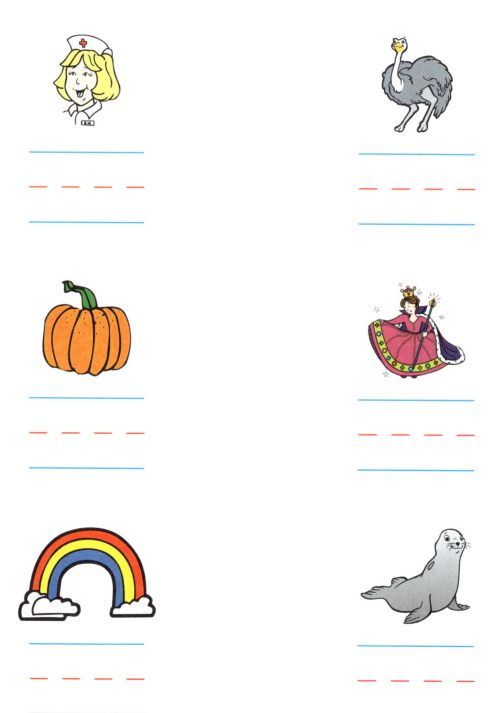

Writing Review

Directions: Say the name of each picture. Write the lowercase letter that names its beginning sound.

Answer Key

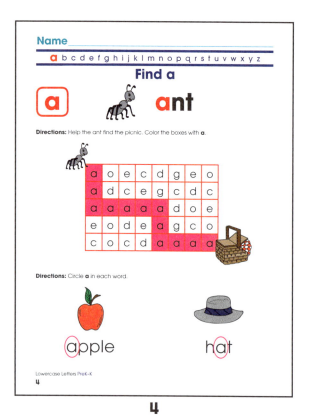

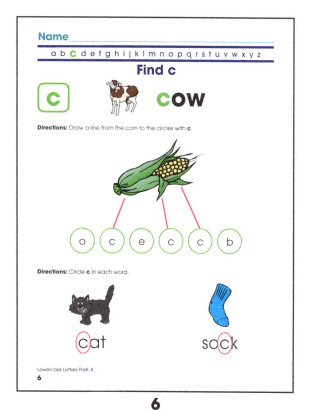

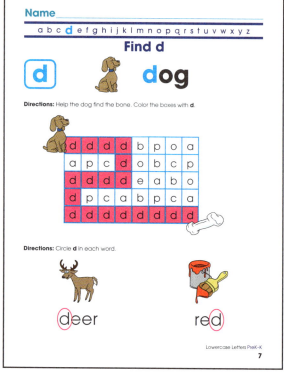

Answer Key

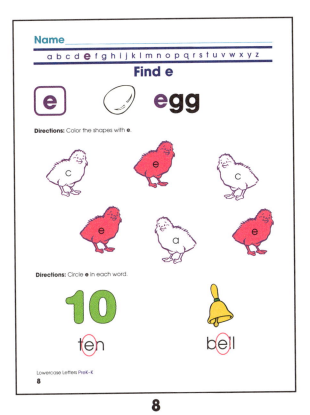

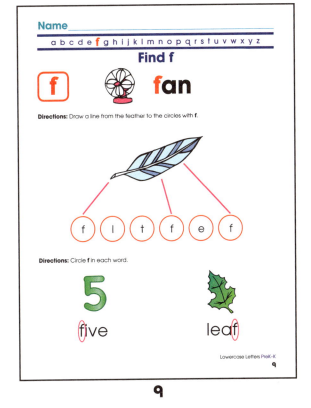

Answer Key

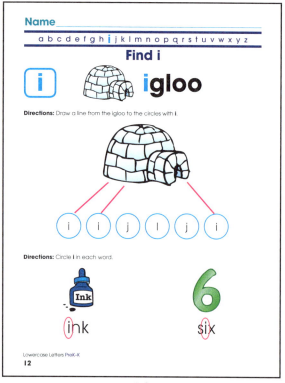

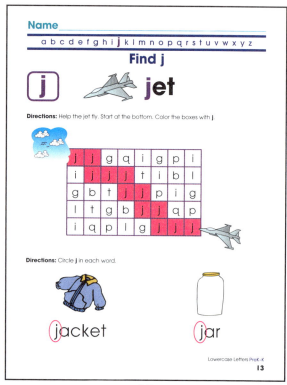

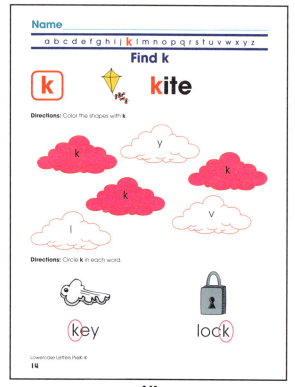

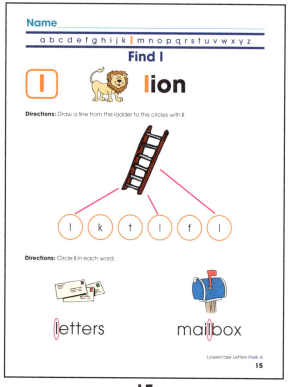

Answer Key

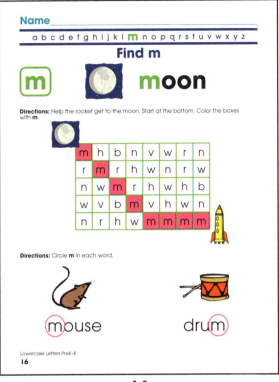

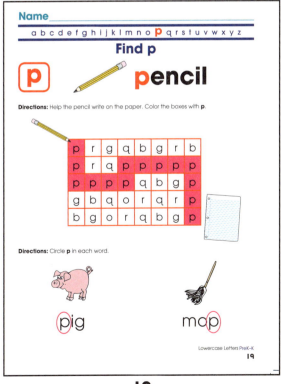

Answer Key

20

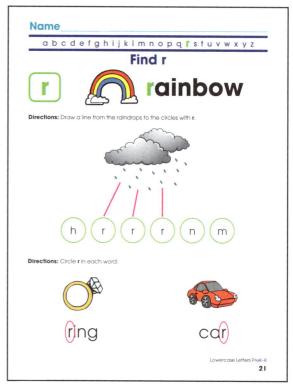

21

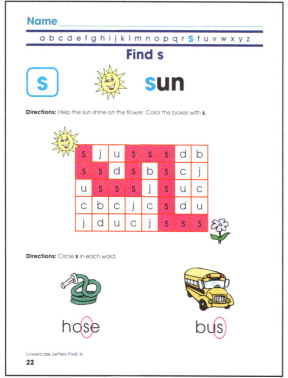

22

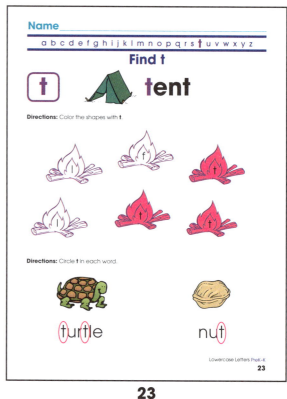

23

Answer Key

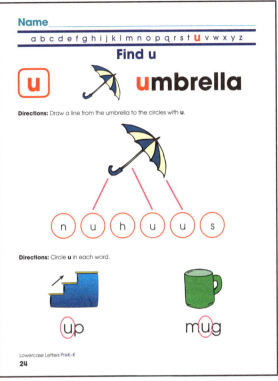

24

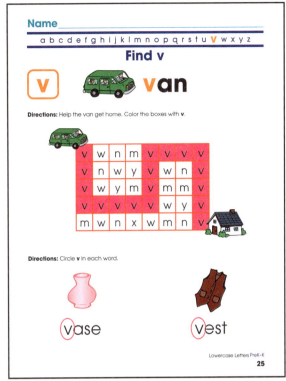

25

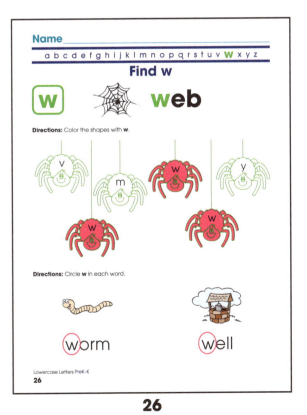

26

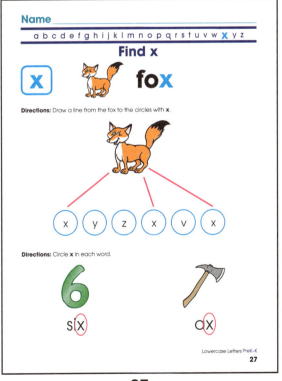

27

Answer Key

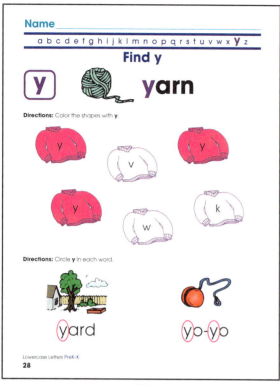

30

31

Answer Key

32

33

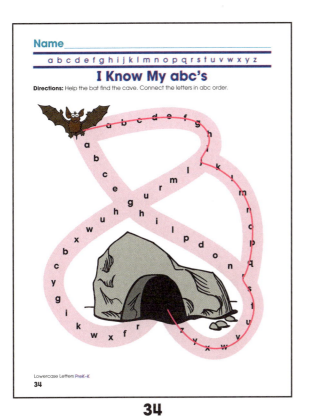

34

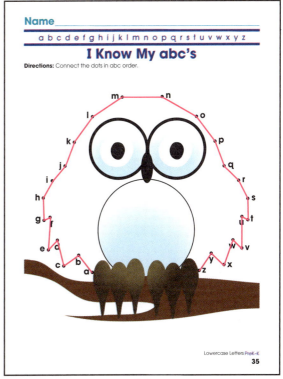

35

Answer Key

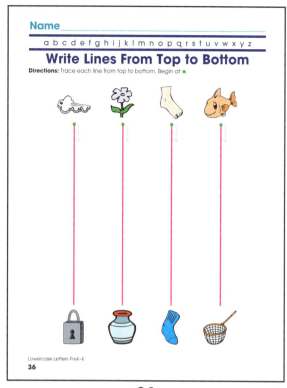

36

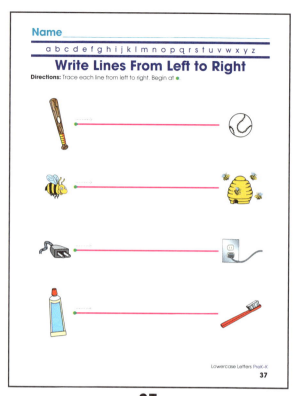

37

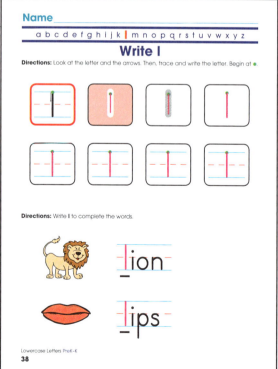

38

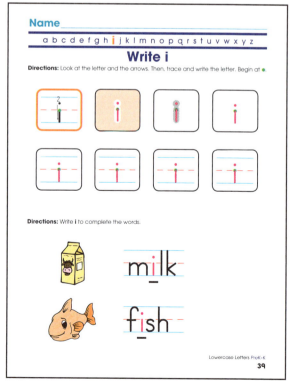

39

Answer Key

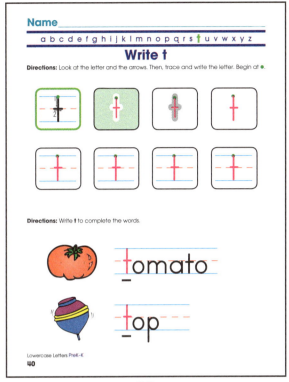

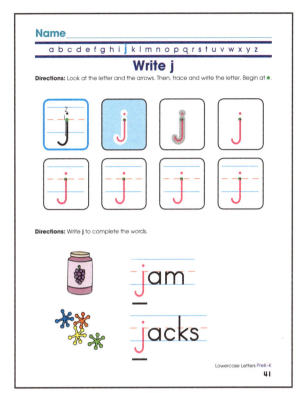

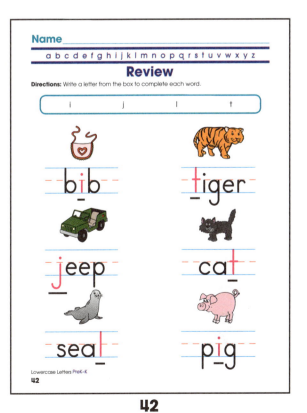

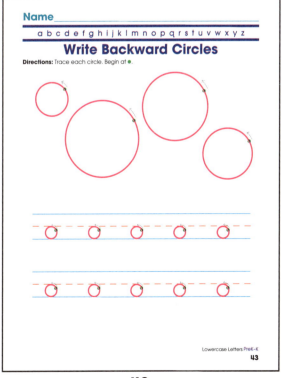

Answer Key

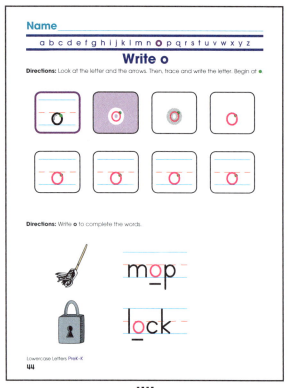

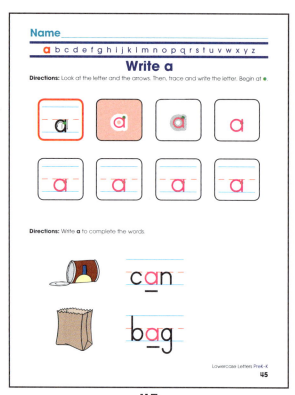

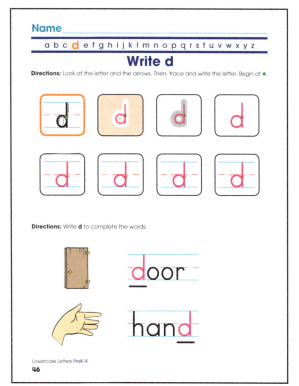

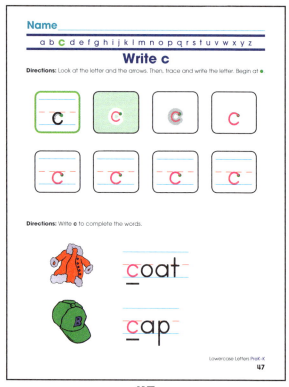

Answer Key

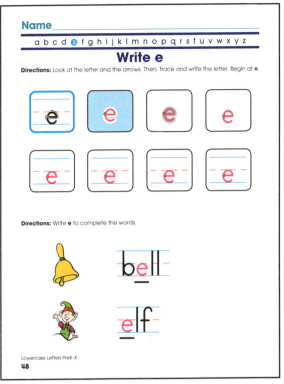

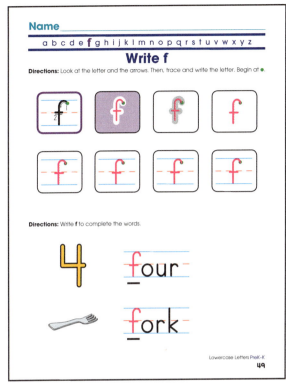

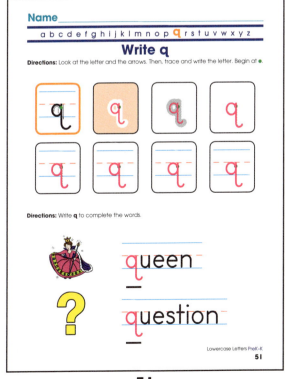

Answer Key

Review

Directions: Write a letter from the box to complete each word.

| a | c | d | e |

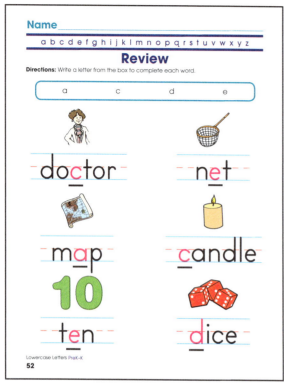

doctor   net

map   candle

10

ten   dice

52

Review

Directions: Write a letter from the box to complete each word.

| f | g | o | q |

goose   goat

quarter   pot

frog   leaf

53

Write Forward Circles

Directions: Trace each circle. Begin at ●.

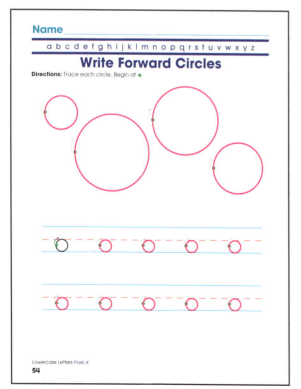

54

Write Curved Lines

Directions: Trace the curved lines. Begin at ●.

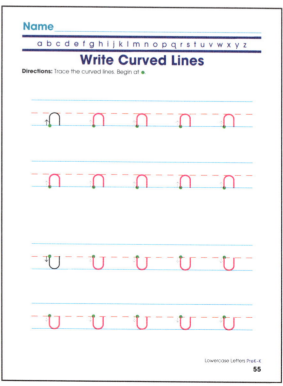

55

Lowercase Letters PreK–K

90

Answer Key

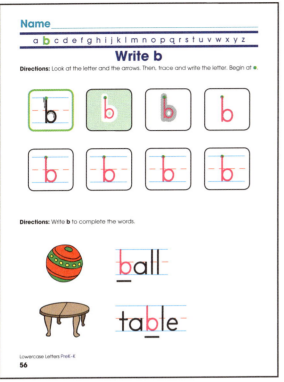

Name

a **b** c d e f g h i j k l m n o p q r s t u v w x y z

Write b

Directions: Look at the letter and the arrows. Then, trace and write the letter. Begin at ●.

Directions: Write **b** to complete the words.

ball

table

Lowercase Letters PreK–K
56

56

Name

a b c d e f g h i j k l m n o **p** q r s t u v w x y z

Write p

Directions: Look at the letter and the arrows. Then, trace and write the letter. Begin at ●.

Directions: Write **p** to complete the words.

pig

pen

Lowercase Letters PreK–K
57

57

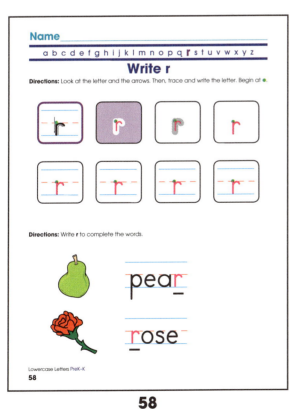

Name

a b c d e f g h i j k l m n o p q **r** s t u v w x y z

Write r

Directions: Look at the letter and the arrows. Then, trace and write the letter. Begin at ●.

Directions: Write **r** to complete the words.

pear

rose

Lowercase Letters PreK–K
58

58

Name

a b c d e f g h i j k l m **n** o p q r s t u v w x y z

Write n

Directions: Look at the letter and the arrows. Then, trace and write the letter. Begin at ●.

Directions: Write **n** to complete the words.

wagon

fan

Lowercase Letters PreK–K
59

59

Answer Key

60

Name_____

a b c d e f g h i j k **l m** n o p q r s t u v w x y z

Write m

Directions: Look at the letter and the arrows. Then, trace and write the letter. Begin at ●.

Directions: Write **m** to complete the words.

mask

ham

Lowercase Letters PreK–K
60

Name_____

a b c d e f **g h** i j k l m n o p q r s t u v w x y z

Write h

Directions: Look at the letter and the arrows. Then, trace and write the letter. Begin at ●.

Directions: Write **h** to complete the words.

hook

horn

Lowercase Letters PreK–K
61

61

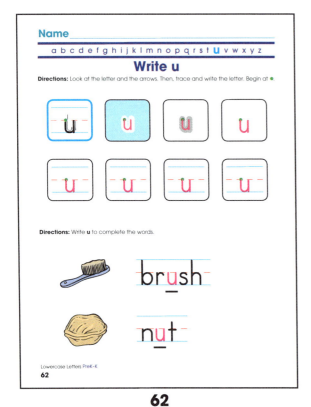

Name_____

a b c d e f g h i j k l m n o p q r s **t u** v w x y z

Write u

Directions: Look at the letter and the arrows. Then, trace and write the letter. Begin at ●.

Directions: Write **u** to complete the words.

brush

nut

Lowercase Letters PreK–K
62

62

Name_____

a b c d e f g h i j k l m n o p q r **s** t u v w x y z

Write s

Directions: Look at the letter and the arrows. Then, trace and write the letter. Begin at ●.

Directions: Write **s** to complete the words.

octopus

seven

Lowercase Letters PreK–K
63

63

Answer Key

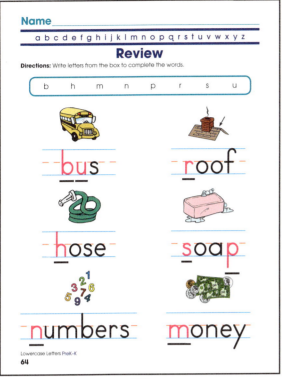

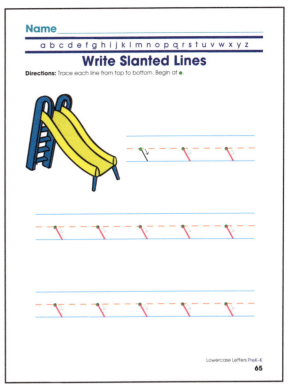

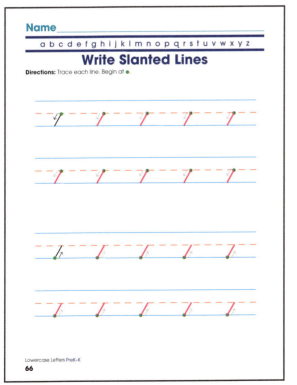

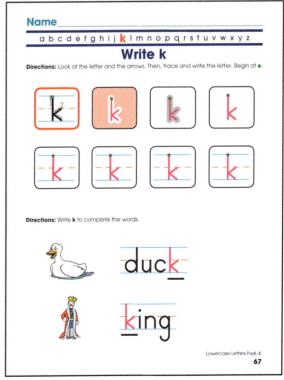

Answer Key

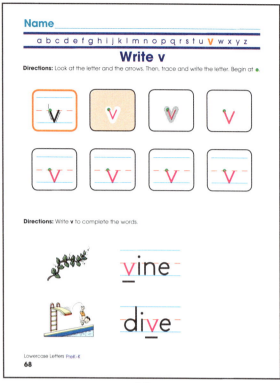

68

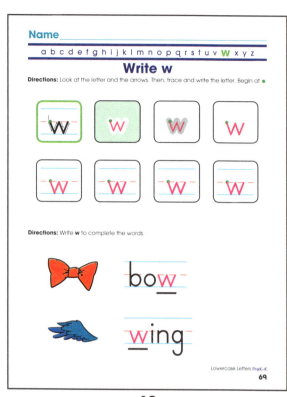

69

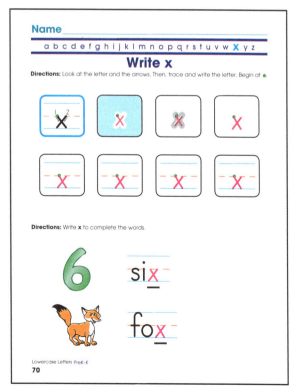

70

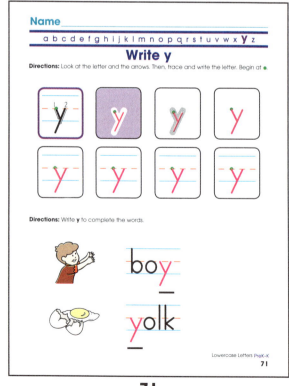

71

Answer Key

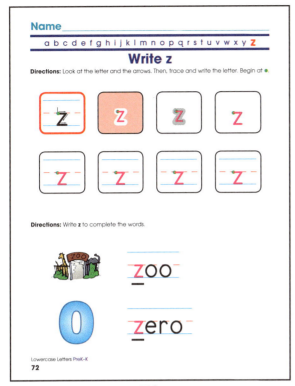

Write z

Directions: Look at the letter and the arrows. Then, trace and write the letter. Begin at ●.

Directions: Write **z** to complete the words.

zoo

zero

72

Review

a b c d e f g h i j k l m n o p q r s t u v w x y z

Directions: Write letters from the box to complete the words.

| k | v | w | x | y | z |

van

zipper

box

yarn

sock

worm

73

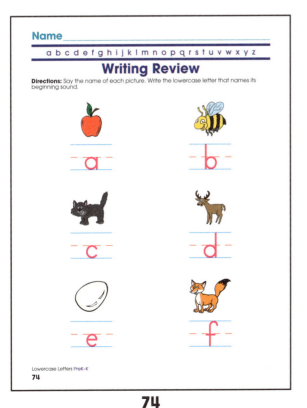

Writing Review

a b c d e f g h i j k l m n o p q r s t u v w x y z

Directions: Say the name of each picture. Write the lowercase letter that names its beginning sound.

a   b

c   d

e   f

74

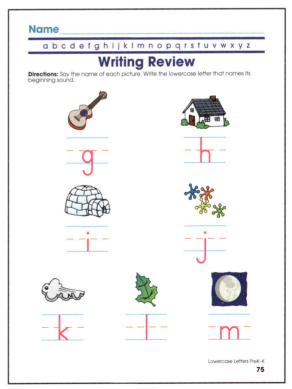

Writing Review

a b c d e f g h i j k l m n o p q r s t u v w x y z

Directions: Say the name of each picture. Write the lowercase letter that names its beginning sound.

g   h

i   j

k   l   m

75

Answer Key

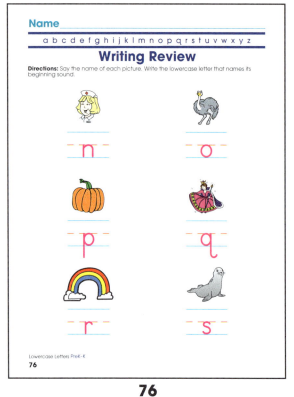

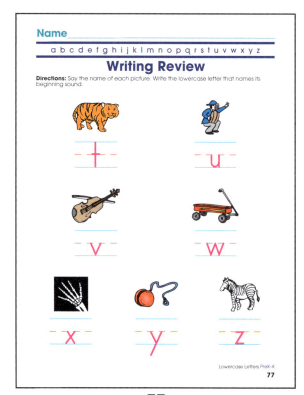